ALCATRAZ

Natalie Hyde

Crabtree Publishing Company
www.crabtreebooks.com

Crabtree Publishing Company

www.crabtreebooks.com

Author: Natalie Hyde
Publishing plan research and development:
Sean Charlebois, Reagan Miller
Crabtree Publishing Company
Photo research: Sonya Newland
Editors: Sonya Newland, Kathy Middleton
Proofreader: Crystal Sikkens
Design: Basement68
Cover design: Ken Wright
Production coordinator and prepress technician: Ken Wright
Print coordinator: Katherine Berti

Produced for Crabtree Publishing by
White-Thomson Publishing

Photographs:
Alamy: D. Alderman: pp. 24–25; Ron Niebrugge: pp. 28–29; Moviestore Collection Ltd: pp. 36–37; **Corbis:** Bettmann: p. 6, 12–13, 16–17, 18, 20, 23, 26–27, 30, 32–33, 36, 38, 39, 40–41; Ted Streshinsky: pp. 8–9; Michael Maloney/San Francisco Chronicle: pp. 44–45; **Dreamstime:** Chenyun Fan: pp. 3, 10–11; CJ08: p. 7; Christian De Grandmaison: p. 9; Hectorshcnz: p. 31; Radekdrewek: p. 35; **FBI:** p. 14; **Flickr:** Digital Sextant: p. 25; **Getty Images:** pp. 14–15; Time & Life Pictures: pp. 34–35; **Press Association:** AP Images: p. 42; **Shutterstock:** Corepics VOF: front cover; David Orcea: back cover; topseller: pp. 1, 4–5; Albo: pp. 20–21; kenkistler: pp. 22–23; Ritu Manoj Jethani: p. 43; **Wikipedia:** U.S. National Archives: p 19; U.S. National Parks Service: p. 29.

Library and Archives Canada Cataloguing in Publication

Hyde, Natalie, 1963-
  Alcatraz / Natalie Hyde.

(Crabtree chrome)
Issued also in electronic formats.
ISBN 978-0-7787-1098-1(bound).--ISBN 978-0-7787-1104-9 (pbk.)

    1. United States Penitentiary, Alcatraz Island, California--
History--Juvenile literature. 2. Prisons--California--Alcatraz
Island--History--Juvenile literature. 3. Alcatraz Island (Calif.)--
History--Juvenile literature. I. Title. II. Series: Crabtree chrome

HV9474.A53H93 2013   j365'.979461   C2012-908183-3

Library of Congress Cataloging-in-Publication Data

Hyde, Natalie, 1963-
 Alcatraz / Natalie Hyde.
     pages cm. -- (Crabtree chrome)
  Includes index.
  ISBN 978-0-7787-1098-1 (reinforced library binding : alk. paper) -- ISBN 978-0-7787-1104-9 (pbk. : alk. paper) -- ISBN (invalid) 978-1-4271-9240-0 (electronic pdf) -- ISBN 978-1-4271-9164-9 (electronic html)
  1. United States Penitentiary, Alcatraz Island, California--History--Juvenile literature. 2. Prisons--California--Alcatraz Island--History--Juvenile literature. 3. Alcatraz Island (Calif.)-- History--Juvenile literature. I. Title.

HV9474.A4H93 2013
365'.979461--dc23
                                            2012047919

Crabtree Publishing Company

www.crabtreebooks.com   1-800-387-7650

Printed in Canada/012013/MA20121217

Published in Canada
Crabtree Publishing
616 Welland Ave.
St. Catharines, ON
L2M 5V6

Published in the United States
Crabtree Publishing
PMB 59051
350 Fifth Avenue, 59th Floor
New York, New York 10118

Published in the United Kingdom
Crabtree Publishing
Maritime House
Basin Road North, Hove
BN41 1WR

Published in Australia
Crabtree Publishing
3 Charles Street
Coburg North
VIC 3058

Contents

The Rock 4

Welcome to Alcatraz 8

Famous Inmates 14

Prison Life 20

Escape from Alcatraz 30

Closing the Doors 42

Learning More 46

Glossary 47

Index 48

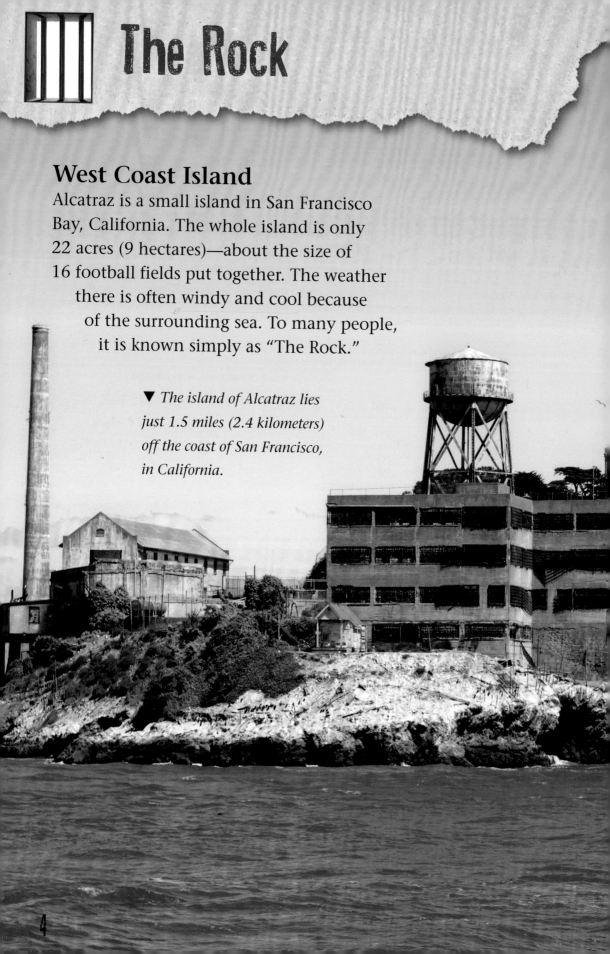

The Rock

West Coast Island

Alcatraz is a small island in San Francisco Bay, California. The whole island is only 22 acres (9 hectares)—about the size of 16 football fields put together. The weather there is often windy and cool because of the surrounding sea. To many people, it is known simply as "The Rock."

▼ *The island of Alcatraz lies just 1.5 miles (2.4 kilometers) off the coast of San Francisco, in California.*

Escape-proof

In 1934, the U.S. government changed a military prison used during the Civil War into a high-security prison on Alcatraz Island. This was going to be a prison for America's most dangerous criminals. Surrounded by **treacherous** waters, Alcatraz was called "escape-proof." No inmate ever did escape and survive … or did they?

The Spanish explorer Juan de Ayala named the island after all the birds he saw there. Alcatraz Island means "Island of the Pelicans."

treacherous: very dangerous

Fort Alcatraz

Before European settlers came, no one lived on Alcatraz Island. The strong currents and cold water made the island hard to reach. Native Americans believed the island was cursed. The first people to stay on Alcatraz Island were soldiers. A fort protected the harbor during the American Civil War. In 1910, a military prison was built.

▼ *In the early 1930s, buildings were added to Alcatraz to make room for more prisoners.*

Alcatraz Prison

Violent crime was on the rise in the U.S. in the 1920s and '30s due to the **Great Depression**. There were many criminal gangs. The government needed a place to punish these dangerous men. The military handed control of Alcatraz over to the U.S. government. The federal prison opened for business in 1934.

Alcatraz Island Light is the oldest lighthouse on the West Coast of the United States. It has survived breakouts, riots, and fires.

▶ *At the base of the lighthouse were rooms where the lighthouse keepers and their families lived.*

Great Depression: a time when many people were unemployed

The Rules of The Rock

Prisoners were taken to The Rock by boat. They wore handcuffs and leg **shackles**. A team of prison guards would meet each new prisoner and explain the strict rules of their new life on Alcatraz Island. Each prisoner was given a copy of the rules so he would not forget them.

▼ *Prisoners had chains on their wrists and ankles to stop them from trying to escape.*

8

A Clean Start

Next, the prisoners were sent to the shower room. They had to give up their clothes and put on a prison uniform. They were given a kit that contained a razor, soap, toothpaste, and a toothbrush. Prisoners could not keep the razor in their cells in case they used it as a weapon.

▲ *This is the clothing issue room in Alcatraz, where prisoners were given their blue and white uniform.*

The Alcatraz uniform was a light blue shirt, blue and white pants, and a web belt with a prisoner number stenciled on it.

shackles: chains that bind a prisoner's wrists or ankles

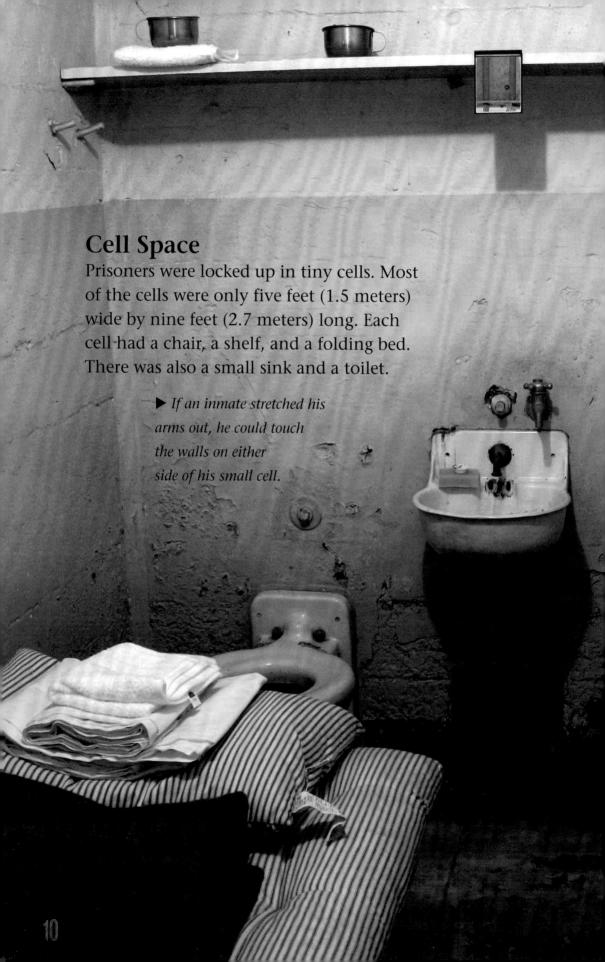

Cell Space

Prisoners were locked up in tiny cells. Most of the cells were only five feet (1.5 meters) wide by nine feet (2.7 meters) long. Each cell had a chair, a shelf, and a folding bed. There was also a small sink and a toilet.

▶ *If an inmate stretched his arms out, he could touch the walls on either side of his small cell.*

Home Sweet Home

Prisoners were allowed a few personal items in their cells. Many of them had musical instruments, books, and art supplies. They were not allowed to have food in their cells except at Christmas. Then, each prisoner got a box of candy as a treat.

"You are entitled to food, clothing, shelter, and medical attention. Anything else is a **privilege**."

James Johnston, warden of
Alcatraz Prison from 1934 to 1948

 privilege: a right or advantage you may have but others do not

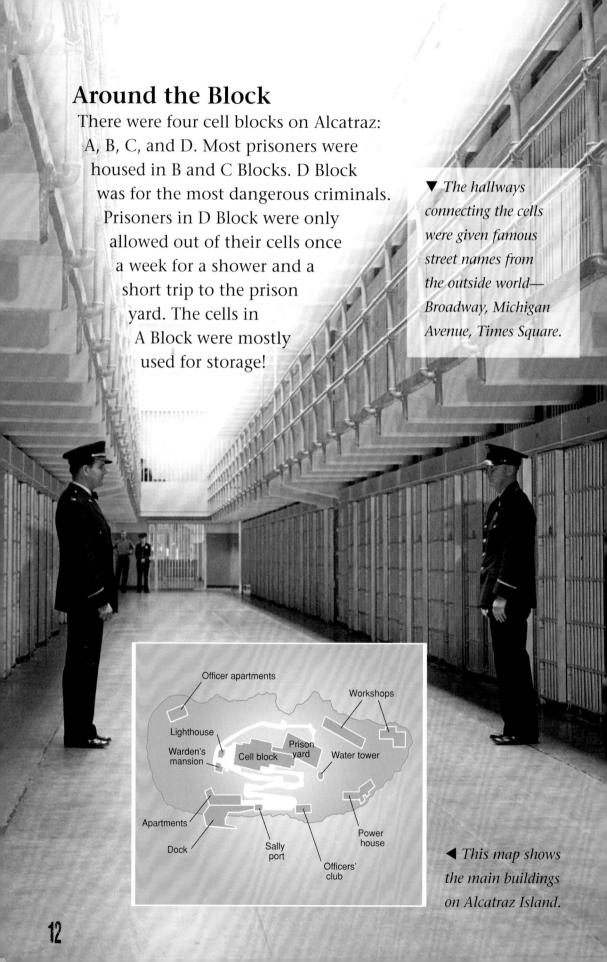

Around the Block

There were four cell blocks on Alcatraz: A, B, C, and D. Most prisoners were housed in B and C Blocks. D Block was for the most dangerous criminals. Prisoners in D Block were only allowed out of their cells once a week for a shower and a short trip to the prison yard. The cells in A Block were mostly used for storage!

▼ *The hallways connecting the cells were given famous street names from the outside world— Broadway, Michigan Avenue, Times Square.*

Officer apartments

Workshops

Lighthouse

Warden's mansion

Cell block

Prison yard

Water tower

Apartments

Dock

Sally port

Officers' club

Power house

◄ *This map shows the main buildings on Alcatraz Island.*

The Hole

Inmates who misbehaved at Alcatraz were sent to solitary confinement also known as "The Hole." The Hole was steel-lined rooms that did not let in any light or sound. During the long days of darkness and silence in The Hole, some prisoners would do simple activities over and over to keep their minds sharp. One inmate used to throw a button from his uniform on the floor and try to find it in the dark.

Under the cell blocks were many old rooms from the days of the military fort. Used as dungeons, these damp, cold, dark rooms housed troublesome inmates or ones who tried to escape. The dungeons were eventually closed in 1942.

 dungeons: underground rooms used as a place of punishment

Famous Inmates

Al Capone

Alphonse "Al" Capone was a famous gangster. He and his men ran all kinds of illegal businesses. They were also suspected of murder. But Capone was never jailed for these crimes. What finally earned him time in a cell was not paying his taxes. He was sentenced to 11 years in prison.

▲ Capone was one of the first inmates to arrive at Alcatraz Prison when it opened in 1934.

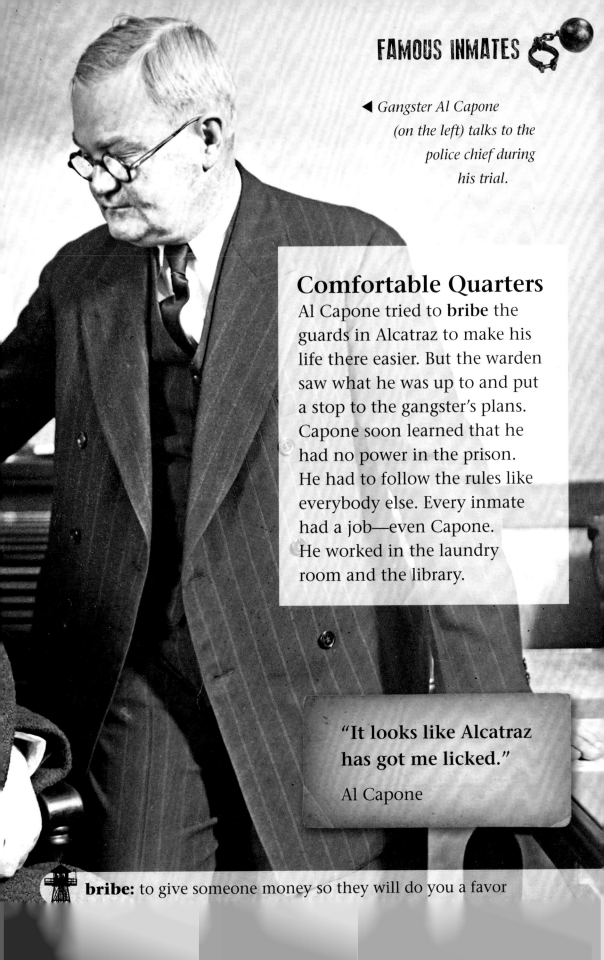

◄ *Gangster Al Capone (on the left) talks to the police chief during his trial.*

Comfortable Quarters

Al Capone tried to **bribe** the guards in Alcatraz to make his life there easier. But the warden saw what he was up to and put a stop to the gangster's plans. Capone soon learned that he had no power in the prison. He had to follow the rules like everybody else. Every inmate had a job—even Capone. He worked in the laundry room and the library.

> "It looks like Alcatraz has got me licked."
>
> Al Capone

bribe: to give someone money so they will do you a favor

George "Machine Gun" Kelly

In 1933, George Kelly Barnes and his gang kidnapped a rich oil **tycoon**. They said they would only free him if they were given $200,000. This was a huge amount of money at the time! Kelly got the cash, but he was later caught and sent to prison for life.

Model Prisoner

While at Alcatraz, Kelly never got in trouble.
He even served as altar boy in the prison chapel.
He often confessed to crimes he never did.
Other inmates thought he wasn't tough at all!
They called him "Pop Gun Kelly."

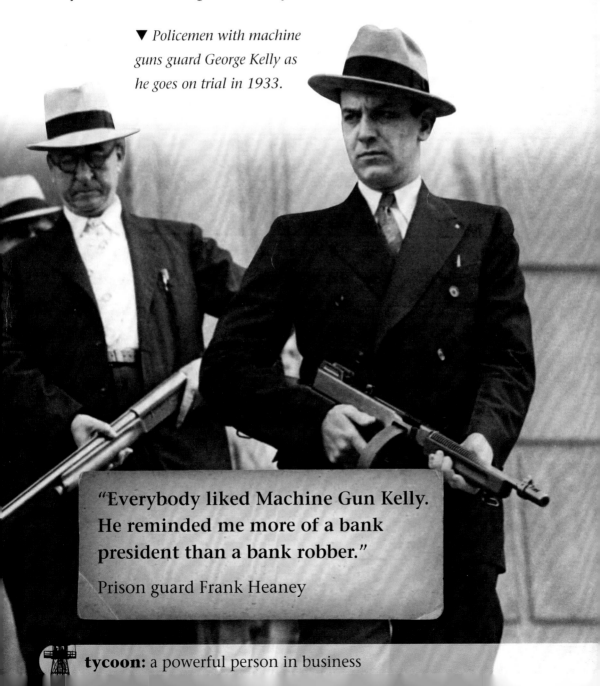

▼ *Policemen with machine guns guard George Kelly as he goes on trial in 1933.*

"Everybody liked Machine Gun Kelly. He reminded me more of a bank president than a bank robber."

Prison guard Frank Heaney

tycoon: a powerful person in business

The Birdman of Alcatraz

Robert Stroud shot and killed a man. He confessed to the crime and was sent to prison in Washington State. While there he became angry and violent. He stabbed another inmate and killed a guard. He was sentenced to be **executed**, but this did not happen. Instead he was sent to Alcatraz for life.

▲ *This is a scene from a movie that was made about the "Birdman" of Alcatraz in 1962.*

Feathered Friends

Stroud's only joy was studying birds. While he was in prison in Washington he raised canaries in his cell. This earned him the nickname "Birdman." When he got to Alcatraz he was not allowed to keep birds any more. But he still researched and wrote about them.

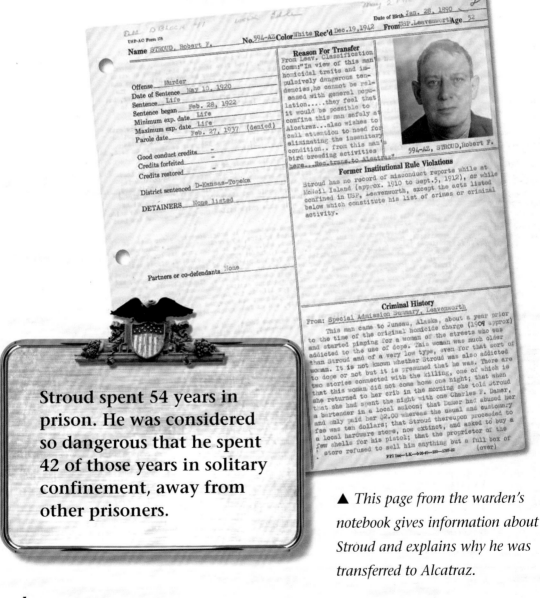

Stroud spent 54 years in prison. He was considered so dangerous that he spent 42 of those years in solitary confinement, away from other prisoners.

▲ *This page from the warden's notebook gives information about Stroud and explains why he was transferred to Alcatraz.*

 executed: to be killed as a punishment for a crime

Prison Life

Rise and Shine

The daily routine at Alcatraz was very strict.
Alarms woke the prisoners at 6:30 a.m. After
breakfast they worked in the **laundry room**, the
gardens, or the prison workshops until 4:10 p.m.
They ate an early supper. At 5:00 p.m., they went
back to their cells for the night. Lights went out
at 9:30 p.m. and the prison would fall silent.

▼ *Some inmates were allowed*
to work in the prison kitchens.

MARCH 13 1956
2 GRILLED FRANKFURTERS
1 HOT CHILI
PARSLEY POTATOES
POT FRIED SAUERKRAUT
BUTTERED CARROTS
1 MUSTARD
1 BANANA PUDDING
2 FRANKFURTER ROLLS

BREAD & TEA

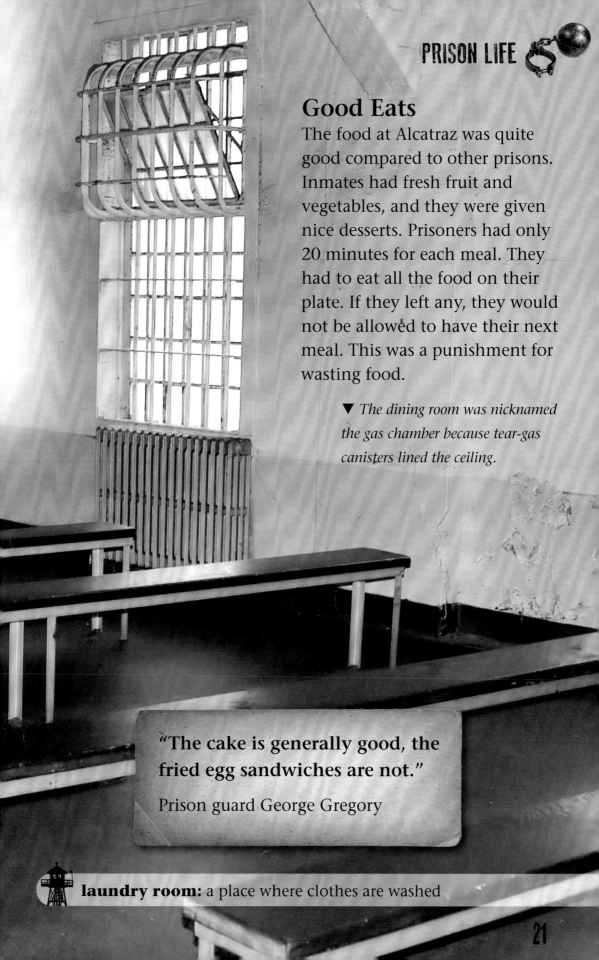

Good Eats

The food at Alcatraz was quite good compared to other prisons. Inmates had fresh fruit and vegetables, and they were given nice desserts. Prisoners had only 20 minutes for each meal. They had to eat all the food on their plate. If they left any, they would not be allowed to have their next meal. This was a punishment for wasting food.

▼ *The dining room was nicknamed the gas chamber because tear-gas canisters lined the ceiling.*

"The cake is generally good, the fried egg sandwiches are not."

Prison guard George Gregory

laundry room: a place where clothes are washed

Work Detail

The workshops at Alcatraz included a glove shop, a shoe shop, a metal shop, and a wood shop. Prisoners who behaved well were allowed to work in these "prison industries." The men were happy to get out of their cells. Sometimes they would get paid for their work. If they worked hard, their **sentence** might even be reduced.

▲ *The workshops were large rooms where inmates would do jobs such as woodwork, metalwork, or sewing.*

Where Are You Going?

Prisoners were sent to the workshops after breakfast. They worked for eight hours. Besides the workshops, men could work in the laundry room, kitchen, office, library, or hospital. Most of them wanted jobs in the workshops. That way they could steal things to help them escape.

▲ *This guard is using a metal detector, which prisoners called the "Snitch Box."*

Many prisoners tried to smuggle metal out of the workshops to make weapons. Every workshop had a metal detector to find items that were being hidden or carried out.

 sentence: a prisoner's punishment that is decided by a judge

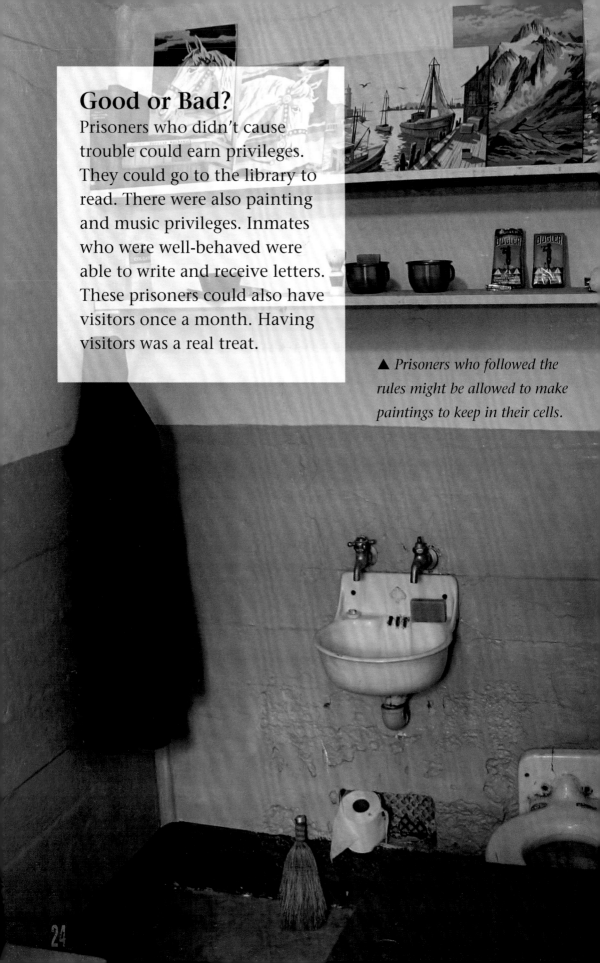

Good or Bad?

Prisoners who didn't cause trouble could earn privileges. They could go to the library to read. There were also painting and music privileges. Inmates who were well-behaved were able to write and receive letters. These prisoners could also have visitors once a month. Having visitors was a real treat.

▲ *Prisoners who followed the rules might be allowed to make paintings to keep in their cells.*

Good to See You!

The prison warden had to **approve** all visitors before they were allowed to see inmates. Prisoners could only visit with family or close friends. They had to sit in separate rooms. They could see each other through a window between the rooms. Inmates spoke to their visitors on a telephone. The guards watched them at all times.

◀ *The rules about having visitors were posted on a large sign in the visitation center.*

"VISITATION RULES & REGULATIONS"
U.S.P., ALCATRAZ

YOU ARE ALLOWED ONE VISIT EACH MONTH FROM MEMBERS OF YOUR IMMEDIATE FAMILY OR OTHER APPROVED VISITORS.

VISITING HOURS ARE APPROXIMATELY 1:30pm - 3:10pm WEEKDAYS.

ALL PERSONAL VISITS YOU WILL CONFINE YOUR TALK TO PERSONAL MATTERS AND REFRAIN FROM DISCUSSING OTHER INMATES, INSTITUTIONAL MATTERS, ETC.

PHYSICAL CONTACT SHALL NOT BE ALLOWED.

FOOD AND BEVERAGES ARE NOT PERMITTED.

INTERVIEWERS AND INMATES SHALL REMAIN SEATED DURING THE VISIT.

INMATES SHALL NOT SMOKE.

VISITS WITH YOUR ATTORNEY OF RECORD MAY BE ARRANGED THROUGH THE OFFICE OF THE ASSOCIATE WARDEN.

VIOLATION OF RULES AND REGULATIONS MAY RESULT IN TERMINATION OF VISITATION ROOM PRIVILEGES.

> **"The first year here wasn't bad—for a prison."**
>
> Darwin Coon, who was sent to Alcatraz in 1959

 approve: to agree to something

The Yard

Inmates looked forward to going to the yard. This was an area outside the cell block surrounded by a high fence. Outside, the men would play sports, such as handball or horseshoes, or just talk with one another. Baseball was **banned** after one prisoner used a bat to hit another! Prisoners also liked to play card games, especially bridge.

▲ *Time spent in the yard was precious to inmates, and they enjoyed the fresh air and exercise.*

Time to Relax

Inside, prisoners would play chess and checkers with other inmates. Every two weeks they had a movie night. They were also allowed a certain time to play musical instruments. Guitars and violins were fine because they were quiet.

Daily newspapers were banned in Alcatraz. The warden did not want prisoners to think about the outside world. Some magazines were allowed, as long as they did not contain articles about crime.

banned: not allowed

Village Life

The prisoners were not the only people who lived on Alcatraz Island. The staff who worked there had homes on the island. The east end of Alcatraz had apartments and cottages. The warden lived in a mansion. The staff had their own corner store and **social club** with a bowling alley. It was like a small village.

▶ *The prison warden lived in a mansion next to the lighthouse. It was burned down in 1970.*

Cool Kids of The Rock

Children lived with their families on Alcatraz, too. They took a ferry across the bay to school each day. On the island there were special rooms where the children could play sports and games. They could go hiking or they might fish in the sea.

▲ *These children are playing on an old cannon, left over from the days when Alcatraz was a fort.*

Children living on Alcatraz were not allowed any contact with the prisoners. They never saw the inside of the prison until the day it closed.

social club: a place to meet and play games with others

Escape from Alcatraz

No Way Out

Alcatraz was called an "escape-proof" prison. The windows were all covered in iron bars. Prisoners were alone in their cells so there was not much chance to plot an escape together. Guards counted the prisoners 13 times each day to make sure everyone was there.

▲ *This guard is operating the cell control panel, which locked the steel cell doors by remote control.*

Nowhere to Go

Security was tight outside the buildings, too. Fences with sharp wire surrounded the cell block. The guards in the watchtowers and outside the cell block had guns and dogs. The sea around the island was deadly cold year round—no one would survive long in the water.

◄ *Guards manned four tall towers that looked out over all parts of the small island.*

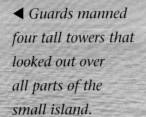

The guards told prisoners there were man-eating sharks in the waters around Alcatraz. This wasn't true, but it was a good way to stop inmates from trying to escape by swimming to shore!

security: a plan to keep things safe

All Planned Out

Escape was next to impossible. First, prisoners would have had to find a way of getting out of the cell block. Guards were watching all the time. The inmates would be missed before they could get very far. Even if they made it outside, they would have to reach the water and swim to shore.

▶ *Even if prisoners escaped from the cell block, it was a long, cold swim to the mainland.*

Try, Try Again

Despite all the security, some foolish prisoners did try to break out of Alcatraz. Over the years, 34 men attempted escape. Nineteen of them were quickly captured again. They were the lucky ones. Nine others were shot and killed. One drowned. Five others disappeared into the bay and were never seen again.

The pelicans on the island were the best guards! These birds do not like to be disturbed, so if someone ran by them, they would make a lot of noise and **alert** the prison guards.

alert: to make someone aware of what's going on

The Battle of Alcatraz

In 1946, six men tried to escape from Alcatraz and failed in the most bloody of the attempts. The escaping prisoners overpowered some guards and got into the room where the guns were stored. They also got the guards' keys. The keys didn't have the one that opened the outside door, however. This **enraged** one of the prisoner's who shot eight of the guards they had locked up in the cells.

▼ *These journalists and photographers are watching to see what happens on Alcatraz during the riots in 1946.*

The End of the Riot

The warden called in the U.S. marines, who attacked the trapped prisoners for two days. A shootout ended the standoff. Two officers and three of the prisoners died. Two other prisoners were later executed.

▲ One of the prisoners used a homemade "bar spreader" to get into the room where the guns were stored.

During one escape attempt, five prisoners made it out of the cell block and to the water's edge. They were caught trying to make a raft with their clothes. They were brought back to the prison naked!

 enraged: to become very angry

The Great Escape

The most daring escape was plotted by four men in 1962. Frank Morris, Allen West, and brothers Clarence and John Anglin wanted to be the first men to escape from Alcatraz. Three of them had already tried to escape from other prisons. That was why they had been sent to The Rock.

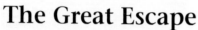

▶ *Clarence Anglin, John Anglin, and Frank Morris made a daring escape from the prison in June 1962.*

▲ *Clint Eastwood played prisoner Frank Morris in the movie* Escape from Alcatraz.

The Plan

It took the men seven months to collect everything they needed. They planned to scrape a hole in the **vents** of their cells. They would crawl out of the building and use a homemade raft to cross the bay. Once in San Francisco, they would steal clothes and a car and make their escape.

The story of this breakout from the "escape-proof" prison was so exciting that it was made into a film starring Clint Eastwood.

vents: openings cut into walls to let air flow through

▲ *Guards checked the cells regularly, so the men had to be on the lookout all the time they were scraping the holes.*

Supplies

The men collected a lot of raincoats—if the other inmates refused to give up their coats, the plotters just stole them. They glued the raincoats together to make a raft and life vests. The men sharpened spoons to scrape the cement walls so they could get into the vents. Fake cardboard vent covers hid the holes.

Getting Ahead

All prisoners were counted at night, so the men had to fool the guards. They made fake heads to put in their beds. Blankets covered most of the faces. The heads looked so real that the guards didn't notice that the men were missing until the morning.

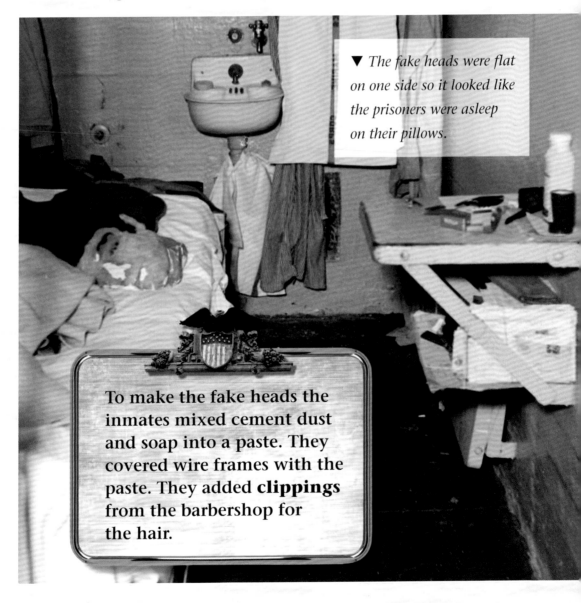

▼ *The fake heads were flat on one side so it looked like the prisoners were asleep on their pillows.*

To make the fake heads the inmates mixed cement dust and soap into a paste. They covered wire frames with the paste. They added **clippings** from the barbershop for the hair.

 clippings: little pieces of hair that fall to the floor during a haircut

Tunneling Out

At 9:30 p.m., after lights out, the men crawled through the holes and up to the roof. Allen West was not there. His hole was too small and he could not squeeze through. By the time he had made the hole big enough and climbed onto the roof it was too late—the others had gone.

Where Are They Now?

The Anglin brothers and Morris climbed up a drainpipe to the roof of the building and made it down to the bay. The **tide** was strong that night. The water was bitterly cold. Bits of their raft were found in the bay, but the men were never seen again. No one knows for sure if they made it or not.

◀ *This guard is looking at the small hole that the prisoners escaped through in June 1962.*

"I can't see how the men could be alive. If the men tried swimming ... they must have drowned within a few moments."

Warden Johnston

 tide: the rise and fall of the oceans

Closing the Doors

The End of the Line

By 1963, the government was looking at its prison system in a new way. There was a push to **rehabilitate** criminals instead of just punishing them. By then, the buildings on Alcatraz were getting old. It would take a lot of money to fix everything. Robert Kennedy, the U.S. Attorney General at the time, decided to close Alcatraz Prison.

◄ *The last inmates of Alcatraz left in March 1963. They were sent to other prisons.*

Alcatraz World

Over 29 years of operation, 1,500 prisoners passed through the doors of Alcatraz. Today, the prison is a tourist attraction. More than one million people visit Alcatraz each year. Visitors can go inside the cell block and see what life was like for prisoners.

▼ *Today, the National Park Service takes care of Alcatraz Island and the buildings on it.*

In 1969, a group of 79 people went to Alcatraz Island and claimed it on behalf of all Native Americans. Their protest lasted nine months. Each year, in honor of that protest, a celebration of the rights of Native peoples is held on Alcatraz. It is known as Unthanksgiving Day.

 rehabilitate: to help someone live a useful life again

Ghostly Inmates

Many men died violent deaths on Alcatraz. Some people believe that their spirits haunt the prison. Security guards and visitors claim to have heard moans and cries coming from the hallways. Some people smell smoke or hear **banjo** music when no one is there.

Alcatraz Lives On

Each year many swimmers join in a race from Alcatraz to the shore. They try to recreate the swim of the men from the great escape in 1962. There have also been many movies made about Alcatraz, its famous inmates, and the daring escape attempts.

▼ *Every year people take part in the "Escape from Alcatraz" swim. They wear wetsuits to protect them from the cold water.*

"To this day, I can't sleep without a light on."

Joyce Ritz, daughter of an officer on Alcatraz who grew up on the island

banjo: a stringed instrument with a long neck and round body

Learning More

Books

Alcatraz Prison
by Marilyn Tower Oliver
(Enslow Publishers, 1998)

Children of Alcatraz
by Clair Murphy
(Bloomsbury US, 2006)

Cornerstones of Freedom:
Alcatraz
by Linda George
(Children's Press, 1999)

Life on Alcatraz
by Judith Janda Presnall
(Lucent Books, 2000)

Mysteries Unwrapped:
The Secrets of Alcatraz
by Susan Sloate
(Sterling, 2008)

Websites

www.nps.gov/alca/index.htm
National Park Service:
Alcatraz Official Website

www.cr.nps.gov/museum/
exhibits/alca/overview.html
National Park Service:
Online Museum Collections

www.alcatrazhistory.com/
mainpg.htm
Alcatraz History

www.alcatrazalumni.org
Pictures and videos
from Alcatraz

Glossary

alert To make someone aware of what's going on

approve To agree to something

banjo A stringed instrument with a long neck and round body

banned Not allowed

bribe To give someone money so they will do you a favor

clippings Little pieces of hair that fall to the floor during a haircut

dungeons Underground rooms used as a place of punishment

enraged Very angry

executed To be killed as a punishment for a crime

Great Depression A time when many people were unemployed

laundry room A place where clothes are washed

privilege A right or advantage you may have but others do not

rehabilitate To help someone live a useful life again

security A plan to keep things safe

sentence A prisoner's punishment that is decided by a judge

shackles Chains that bind a prisoner's wrists or ankles

social club A place to meet and play games with others

tide The rise and fall of the oceans

treacherous Very dangerous

tycoon A powerful person in business

vents Openings cut into walls to let air flow through

Index

Entries in **bold** refer to pictures

Anglin, Clarence 36, **36**, 41
Anglin, John 36, **36**, 41
Ayala, Juan de 5

Barnes, George "Machine Gun" Kelly 16–17, **16–17**
Battle of Alcatraz 34–35, **34–35**, 35

Capone, Al 14–15, **14–15**, **15**
cell blocks 12, **12–13**, 13, 26, 31, 32, 35, **42**, 43
cells 10, **10–11**, 11, 20, 22, **24–25**, 30, 34, 37
children 29, **29**
Christmas 11
Civil War 5, 6
Coon, Darwin 25

daily routine 20
dining room 20–21
dungeons 13

Eastwood, Clint **36–37**, 37
escape attempts 5, 23, 30–41, 45
"Escape from Alcatraz" swim **44–45**, 45

fake heads 39, **39**
food 21

games 26, 27
ghosts of Alcatraz 44
Great Depression 7
Gregory, George 21
guards 8, 15, 17, 18, 21, **23**, 25, 30, **30**, 31, 32, 33, 34, 39, **39**, **40–41**

Heaney, Frank 17
Hole, The 13

Johnston, James 11, 41

Kennedy, Robert 42
kitchens **20**, 23

laundry 15, 20, 23
library 15, 23, 24
lighthouse 7, **7**

magazines 27
Morris, Frank 36, **36**, 41
movies **36–37**, 37, 45
musical instruments 11, 27

Native Americans 6, 43
newspapers 27

pelicans 5, 33
privileges 24

rafts 35, 37, 38
rules 8, 15

security 30, 31, 33
sharks 31
size of Alcatraz 4
Snitch Box 23, **23**
social club 28
sports 26
staff quarters 28
Stroud, Robert "Birdman" **18**, 18–19, **19**

tourism 43

uniform 9, 13

vents 37, 38, **40–41**
visitors 24, 25

warden 11, 15, 25, 27, 28, 35, 41
warden's mansion 28, **28–29**
watchtowers 31, **31**
West, Allen 36, 40
workshops 20, 22, **22–23**, 23

yard 12, 26, **26–27**